RHEILFFORDD FFESTINIOG
FFESTINIOG RAILWAY

Published by the Festiniog Railway Company

Harbour Station, Porthmadog, Gwynedd, LL49 9NF
01766 516024   enquiries@ffwhr.com
www.festrail.co.uk   facebook.com/festrail

Produced by Roy Woods, January 2013
Updated by Richard Buxton and Clare Britton, January 2016

ISBN: 978-0-90 1848-15-4

Above: 'Linda' *and the 'Earl' leave Harbour Station on a sunny February afternoon.* (Roger Dimmick)
Front cover photo: 'Linda' *rounds Tank Curve on the morning service to Blaenau Ffestiniog* (Chris Parry)
Rear Cover photo: *New Observation carriage No.150 leaves the paint shop at Boston Lodge Works* (Glenn Williams)

DESIGNED AND PRINTED BY SNOWDONIA DESIGN & PRINT, PORTHMADOG

CROESO !

In 1863 the Ffestiniog Railway began the use of steam locomotives to haul trains of empty slate wagons from the harbour at Porthmadog to the quarries of Blaenau Ffestiniog. Two were named 'Prince' and 'Princess', reflecting widespread public interest in the marriage of the Prince of Wales, the future Edward VII, to Princess Alexandra of Denmark, and one named 'Palmerston' after the then Prime Minister, who was also an investor in one of the Ffestiniog slate quarries.

Built barely more than 30 years after Stephenson's 'Rocket', these George England engines are the oldest surviving narrow gauge locomotives in the world. Remarkably, after 150 years, four of the six built still survive, two of them in regular use, and a third - 'Welsh Pony' - is currently being restored to full working order.

Croeso i Reilffordd Ffestiniog, un o'r rheilffyrdd bach mwyaf adnabyddus ac uchel ei barch yn y byd. Mae trenau ager wedi rhedeg yma am 150 o flynyddoedd, ac yn rhyfeddol, mae rhai o'r locomotifau gwreiddiol dal i fod o gwmpas y rheilffordd heddiw - yn wir, mae hanes o amgylch chi.

Ond un o'r agweddau mwyaf arbennig y rheilffordd yw ysbryd y bobl sydd y tu ôl iddo. Mae llawer o'r staff yr ydych yn gweld o gwmpas y rheilffordd yn wirfoddolwyr.

Maent yn helpu i redeg y trenau drwy wneud swyddi angenrheidiol i sicrhau gweithrediad y rheilffordd. Mae'r rheilffordd yn arbennig iddynt ac yr wyf yn gobeithio y bydd i chi hefyd. Fel gwirfoddolwr fy hun am flynyddoedd lawer, yr wyf yn awr yn falch o fod yn rheolwr ar y llinell bach hyfryd hon, sy'n agos i galon cynifer o bobl.

Cynlluniwyd y llyfr yma i'ch helpu i gael y gorau o'ch ymweliad:

* Yn y canol mae map i chi ddilyn.
* Cewch gwybod mwy am yr hyn y gallwch ei wneud yn ein prif orsafoedd ym Mlaenau Ffestiniog, Porthmadog a Than y Bwlch.
* Ac, ar ôl eich ymweliad, bydd y llyfr a'r lluniau yn eich atgoffa drachen a thrachen am y rheilffordd a'r ardal hardd.

Gobeithio eich bod wedi mwynhau eich ymweliad ac yn gadael gydag atgofion melys.

Clare Britton
Rheolwr Masnachol.

Below: *'Princess' basks in the winter sunshine after being rolled out of the Boston Lodge paintshop in January 2013 - the year of her 150th birthday.*

Chris Parry

WELCOME !

Welcome to the Ffestiniog Railway, one of the most renowned and respected little railways in the World. Steam trains have been running here for 150 years and amazingly, some of those original tiny locomotives are still around the railway today – in fact, there is history all around you.

But one of the most special aspects of the railway is the irrepressible spirit of the people who are behind it. Many of the staff you meet are volunteers, giving up days off and holidays to be a part of the Ffestiniog Family. The railway is special to them and I hope it will be for you too. As a volunteer myself for many years, I am now proud to be a manager of this wonderful little line which captures the hearts of so many.

This book is designed to help you get the most from your visit:

- In the centre is a fold out map for you to follow.
- Learn some fascinating snippets of local history and other attractions in the area.
- Find out more about what you can do from our main stations at Blaenau Ffestiniog, Porthmadog and Tan y Bwlch.
- And, after your visit, this will be a reminder of your trip with some lovely photographs and interesting information about the railway and the beautiful area through which it passes.

We hope you will enjoy your visit and leave with fond memories.

Clare Britton
Commercial Manager.

How many Fs in Ffestiniog?

In the early 19th Century Welsh spelling had not yet been formalised and different spellings from those with which we are familiar today were frequently used for place names. As a result of this, the Act of Parliament which brought the Festiniog Railway Company into being used just one F in Festiniog. This remains the legal title of the Company. Changing it would require another Act of Parliament. The correct modern Welsh spelling of Ffestiniog uses two Fs. The Festiniog Railway Company continued to use just one F for many years. However it now uses the double F spelling for most purposes, only using the single F version where the legal title of the Company is required.

Below: *The Moelwyn mountains and the entrance to Blaenau Ffestiniog station seen through the new slate pillars. The town's regeneration scheme was undertaken in 2012, seeking to celebrate its wealth of heritage but also looking to a new future.*

150 YEARS OF STEAM

The Ffestiniog was the first railway in the world to adopt and make regular use of steam locomotives on a very narrow gauge, on a public railway, and over a significant distance. The introduction of these steam locomotives was a vital first step in the transformation of a well-engineered and well-run horse and gravity mineral railway into a state-of-the-art steam traction system worthy of emulation world-wide.

The introduction of steam locomotives on the Ffestiniog Railway demonstrated that the technology of the steam railway that had evolved on the main lines from 1829 onwards could be applied to railways built on a much smaller scale and at much lower cost. As such it paved the way for further innovations on the Ffestiniog itself, including the introduction of passenger traffic in 1865, for articulated locomotives in 1869 and for the locomotive trials of 1870 which attracted engineers from around the world.

The technology and skills developed on the Ffestiniog were exported around the world and led to the proliferation of narrow gauge railways in other countries where inexpensive and cost-effective systems were required. The narrow gauge railways of France, India, the USA, Hungary, South Africa, Namibia, Venezuela, New Guinea and Morocco – as well as industrial systems and those built in the trenches of the First World War – can all trace their roots back to a 13 mile line in North Wales.

Below: 'Princess' *at Paddington.*

Chris Parry

4

150 YEARS OF PASSENGERS

The Ffestiniog Railway began its passenger services on 5th January 1865, with tiny four-wheeled carriages used to convey its first intrepid travellers. Victorian tourists soon discovered the railway and beautiful, ornate bogie carriages were built to satisfy this new market. As the slate industry declined, visitors replaced the slate traffic and became the mainstay of the line - but those same Victorian carriages remained in use until passenger trains ceased at the outbreak of WW2. Since the re-opening of the line in the 1950s, the increased numbers of visitors to the railway has required the building of new carriages to cope with demand.

However, we have been fortunate to retain many of our original carriages. Heritage Lottery funds have allowed us to return them to their former glory, in a new workshop complete with restoration and training facilities. As a result, the railway now uses a fleet of modern, comfortable carriages - built in our own works by local craftsmen - which cater to the needs of today's visitors. This year, 2016, will see the launch of a new set of carriages, which will take our standards of passenger comfort to an even higher level.

1865 - 2015

150 YEARS OF FFESTINIOG RAILWAY PASSENGER TRAINS

Below Left: *In the 1860s our passengers were carried in these carriages. We still have some original carriages, lovingly restored, whilst others are faithful replicas, built in our workshops.*

Below Right: *From the 1870s to the 1960s our passengers travelled in carriages like this. They are still used regularly to lengthen trains at particularly busy times and at special events.*

Bottom: *Today you are probably travelling in a carriage like this, one of the Company's most modern saloon carriages, designed in-house and built in Boston Lodge works.*

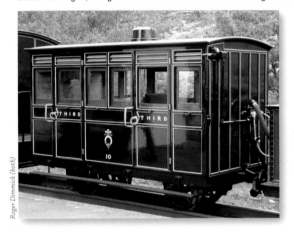

Roger Dimmick (both)

Roger Dimmick

5

A JOURNEY FROM PORTHMADOG TO BLAENAU FFESTINIOG

F/R Archives

William Alexander Madocks

In 1806, William Alexander Madocks constructed a model town on reclaimed land near his house, Tan yr Allt, overlooking the Glaslyn Estuary. Named Tremadog, the town was intended to be the last staging post on a London to Ireland packet route via Porth Dinllaen. The historic centre of the town was complete by 1811, and this part of the town remains substantially unaltered to this day.

The town includes many fine buildings, such as Snowdon Lodge, a Grade II listed building in which T. E. Lawrence, the famous Lawrence of Arabia, was born in 1888. Ty Newydd, (New House), is a 19th century detached house which was once used as a court house and jail.

Porthmadog would never have existed at all without the reclamation works carried out by William Madocks, who named the town after both himself and the Welsh prince Madog, who some say sailed from the nearby Ynys Fadog (Madog's Island) to North America in 1170.

Roy Woods

The £1.1 million project to develop the historic Porthmadog Harbour Station was completed in March 2014. Almost 40,000 tons of fill material and armour stone, obtained from nearby Minffordd Quarry, have been placed to widen 260 metres of the 200 year old Cob.

Harbour Station was originally opened to passengers in 1865. The recent work has enabled the construction of a second platform at the station, making it possible for Ffestiniog and Welsh Highland trains to be in the station at the same time, and for there to be cross platform interchange between the two. The track layout and signalling system provide for considerable operational flexibility in the way the station may be run. All the main line points and signals are electrically operated.

The station redesign means there is much more space on the platform for passengers, and has also made possible the construction of an outdoor area attached to Spooner's where it is possible, on fine days, to sit enjoying food and drink while watching the trains come and go.

The Ffestiniog Railway's Harbour Station is at the southernmost end of Porthmadog High Street, next to the town's harbour. It is well worth while taking some time to walk around the harbour, as there are interesting buildings to admire, many of which are nearly two hundred years old. The 19th century wharves survive, although all but one of the long, low slate storage sheds have now disappeared as most of the dockside areas have been converted to other uses, mostly connected with yachting and other aquatic recreational activity. The one remaining low shed now houses the Maritime Museum. Many of the old warehouses have been turned into holiday apartments, but The Ship (Y Llong) public house in Lombard Street serves as a reminder of earlier days.

Dave Thurlow

Above: *An aerial view of Harbour Station showing the extended footprint as part of the re-development programme. Now this scheme is finished, it allows two trains into the station at the same time.*

Roger Dimmick

If you walk past the boatyards and chandlers you will find a footpath around the headland to Borth y Gest, a delightful little seaside village, about a mile distant.

The station area shows many signs of its development over the years since the railway was first built. The old slate quay opposite, South Snowdon Wharf, is now the site of a 1960s apartment block development, styled as a Mediterranean fishing village. Across the road is a footpath leading up to Ynys Tywyn, a superb vantage point owned by the National Trust.

Top: *Trains to Blaenau Ffestiniog and Caernarfon stand ready to depart either side of the new platform at Harbour Station, April 2014.*

Below: *Beyer-Garratt No.143 steams into Harbour Station from Caernarfon. Spooner's outdoor seating area provides perfect views of arriving and departing trains.*

John Elis-Williams

The Cob

The construction of the Cob, though undertaken primarily as a means of enclosing the Glaslyn estuary, vested in Madocks by an enclosure act, also had important implications for the development of transport. The Cob itself became a roadway connecting Caernarvonshire and Merioneth and figured in Madocks's grand plans for a road from London to a packet port for Ireland at Porthdinllaen on the Llŷn Peninsula.

Its completion in 1811 saw great celebrations, including horse races and the roasting of an ox. Unfortunately, within three weeks, it was breached in a great storm and it took a further three years for it to be fully repaired. Over the years the Cob has withstood many violent storms, but probably the most destructive was one in 1927 which resulted in a further breach which took several months to repair. FR trains ran from Boston Lodge in the meantime.

The Cob has been strengthened on several occasions, most recently during 2001, when the A487 road was also widened and an extension built to carry a pathway for walkers and cyclists.

In 2011 the 200th anniversary of the Cob took place and there was a great celebration in Porthmadog and Minffordd to mark the occasion.

2014 saw the completion of the Cob widening project which has increased the footprint of Harbour Station, thereby allowing both WHR and FR trains to have separate platforms.

A frosty morning highlights the new track layout at Harbour Station, January 2016.

Roger Dimmick

'Blanche' *crosses the Cob on a bright January day in 2010.*

Dave Thurlow

8

As the train leaves Harbour station, it crosses a causeway called the Cob. On your right there are fine views of the estuary. Inland, the magnificent panorama of Snowdonia unfurls with, from left, Moel Hebog, Snowdon, Cnicht, Moelwyn Mawr and Moelwyn Bach, against the skyline. The Glaslyn marshes are home to many species of duck, also curlews, oystercatchers, cormorants, mute swans and little egrets. Other wading birds are also seen frequently. It is also renowned for over-wintering birds. If you are very lucky you may see otters or even a grey seal sneaking upriver in pursuit of salmon!

After a mile the railway turns sharply left on an embankment overlooking the road and the old toll gate, closed in 2003. The railway's workshops are here, at Boston Lodge, and on the right you can see an extensive array of tracks and buildings. Keep a sharp eye out as you may well see one or more of the railway's engines being prepared for duty. Boston Lodge is now a thriving industrial concern, not only maintaining the railway's fleet of carriages, wagons and locomotives, but also building equipment under contract for other companies. These items range from iron gates and ship's propellers to engines and carriages for other railways.

Top: 'Earl of Merioneth' *rounds the curve at Boston Lodge with an Up train, October 2012.*
Below: *Replica Pickering Carriage built for the Welshpool & Llanfair Light Railway.*

Boston Lodge Works

Boston Lodge is the engineering works of the Ffestiniog & Welsh Highland Railways. The present workforce is continuing a long established tradition of innovation and quality stretching back more than 150 years. Heritage locomotives and carriages can be restored and repaired on site whilst we are also able to produce modern locomotives and stock.

Past projects include two vehicles designed and constructed to replicate Darjeeling Himalayan Railway examples and the construction of three replica Pickering carriages for the Welshpool & Llanfair Light Railway.

London Transport Museum's unique Metropolitan Railway first class Jubilee Carriage number 353, built in 1892 for the world's first underground railway, has been restored by craftsmen at Boston Lodge Works. The gleaming carriage, finished with gold leaf and carrying no fewer than 12 coats of varnish, underwent a painstaking 15-month restoration to celebrate 150 years of the London Underground.

Roger Dimmick

Old Locomotive Shed

Built in 1863, the old locomotive shed is an iconic piece of the railway's heritage. It has been recently restored to its original condition by local craftsmen and, in 2009, won The Network Rail Partnership Award, presented by Lord Adonis, then Secretary of State for Transport.

The F&WHR Trust, financed by bequests from Ffestiniog Railway Society members Norman Gurley and Rodney Weaver, provided the majority of the funding, with top ups from the Trust funds, the FR Society and CADW.

Roger Dimmick

Roger Dimmick

On the hillside above Boston Lodge is Plas Penrhyn. This house, with its beautiful ornate verandah affording views towards the Llŷn and Snowdon, was originally the home of Samuel Holland, one of the promoters of the Ffestiniog Railway. It was often visited by his cousin Elizabeth Gaskell, the famous Victorian novelist. In more recent years it has been home to Bertrand Russell, the philosopher, best known for his work in mathematical logic and for his social and political campaigns, including his advocacy of both pacifism and nuclear disarmament. He received the Nobel Prize for Literature in 1950. Russell is one of a number of internationally-famous academics who have lived in the area – including Lord Patrick Blackett, winner of a Nobel Prize for Physics, a close friend of Russell, and Arthur Koestler CBE, the Hungarian-born novelist, journalist and critic, well known for his novel Darkness at Noon.

At Boston Lodge, the old locomotive shed has been rebuilt to its original Victorian glory, in an award winning project led by the Ffestiniog and Welsh Highland Railways Trust. This now provides a safe haven for our newly restored vintage carriage fleet. There is a halt here, from which there is a footpath over the peninsula to Portmeirion. Leaving Boston Lodge, the train passes very close to a house and if you look very carefully, you'll notice that the garage is located on an old turntable!

Below: 'Linda' *and* 'Merddin Emrys' *at Boston Lodge Halt with a train for Porthmadog, October 2012.*

Oliver Bennett

A short tunnel, Rhiw Plas bridge, follows as we pass under the main road and start to climb inland. On the left is the village cemetery and one of the area's still-busy quarries, the Garth Quarry, which started with the production of granite setts, or cobblestones, in 1870. Amongst other products, it now provides ballast for the FR and supplied the stone for the Cob widening.

After the level crossing we enter Minffordd, passing the railway's main hostel, constructed in the 1990s to house volunteers. The large area on the left is the old interchange yard where slate was transhipped onto the main line. It is now home to the Railway's Infrastructure Department, new workshops and storage facilities, and a major new building designed to house undercover the Railway's large collection of slate waggons and other historic goods vehicles. We pass over the bridge across the old Cambrian Railways main line as we enter Minffordd station, which is the place to disembark if you wish to visit Portmeirion.

Minffordd is a crossing point on the single line and most days trains pass each other here. There is also a small water tank to replenish a locomotive's supply if necessary.

As the train leaves Minffordd, it crosses a new bridge over the Porthmadog by-pass, constructed in 2011. On the right is the old Bron y Garth hospital, now replaced by Ysbyty Alltwen on the outskirts of Porthmadog on the road to Caernarfon. Bron y Garth was formerly the Ffestiniog Union Workhouse.

Top: 'Blanche' *approaches Minffordd with a train for Blaenau Ffestiniog - viewed from the chimney stack on top of the station house roof.*

Below: 'Linda' *and* 'Taliesin' *steam into Minffordd station with an early season train, March 2014.*

The Cambrian Coast Line

One of the most scenic railway lines in the whole of Britain, the Cambrian Coast Line is a superb way to explore the beautiful and varied Gwynedd coastline. Discover busy seaside resorts, tiny coastal villages, steam railways, vast sandy beaches and no end of views to remember. Trains depart from Minffordd to Pwllheli to the west and Abermaw (Barmouth) and Aberystwyth in the south.

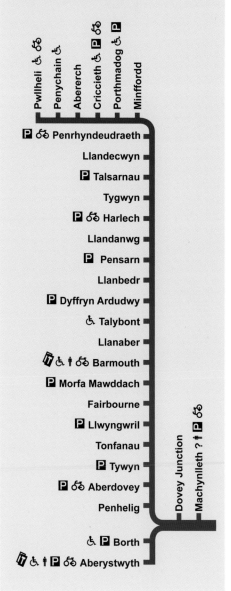

Chris Parry

Pont Briwet.

Pont Briwet is the name given to the combined road and rail bridge which crosses the Dwyryd estuary between Penrhyndeudraeth and Llandecwyn. Originally built in the 1860s for the Cambrian Coast Railway, it was constructed of wood. It carried the single track railway line, and a very narrow privately operated toll road only suitable for motor cars. By the early 2010s the whole structure was clearly life expired.

It has been replaced by a completely new bridge over the last two years, which still carries the single track railway line, together with a widened two lane road open to all vehicles. Travel between the north and south sides of the Dwyryd have thereby been very greatly improved. Amongst other things, the bus route between Barmouth and Harlech has been extended to Porthmadog, thus complimenting the Cambrian Coast train service.

Roger Dimmick

The line climbs steadily on an embankment and curves round the back of the village of Penrhyndeudraeth. Here is Penrhyn station, which retains much of its 19th Century charm, having been lovingly restored by volunteers. There is also a small hostel here for railway volunteers.

Top: 'Merddin Emrys' *passes slowly through Penrhyn station, September 2008.*
Below: 'Blanche' *and* 'Prince' *leave Penrhyn with a train for Blaenau Ffestiniog.*

Roger Dimmick

Chris Parry

Roy Woods

Leaving Penrhyn there are excellent views to the right across the valley and back down the Dwyryd estuary towards Harlech Castle. The train crosses the A4085 road to Llanfrothen and Beddgelert on a level crossing. Don't forget to wave to the crossing keeper, he's usually on your left as you're going up!

Just after the level crossing, the train passes the boundary stone marking entry into the Snowdonia National Park. After the farmhouse on the left there are some adits in the bank, which are the remains of some of the many lead and copper mines which riddle this area. Keeping close to the wall, the train runs through another passing loop, Rhiw Goch.

Top: *With a cheery wave from the driver, 'Taliesin' steams onto Penrhyn crossing, October 2010.*
Below: *'David Lloyd George' passes Rhiw Goch signalbox with a train to Blaenau Ffestiniog, May 2009.*

Dave Thurlow

Penrhyndeudraeth

The name Penrhyndeudraeth means 'Promontory between two beaches'. 'Penrhyn' is promontory, 'deu' is the same as dau, meaning two, and 'draeth' is a form of 'traeth' which is a beach or estuary. Penrhyndeudraeth's origins are fairly recent, and the oldest part of the village is Upper Penrhyn, or Cefn Coch (Red Ridge). The people who lived here in a few cottages would have been mainly employed in agriculture and copper and lead mining. Some men would have worked on boats on the Afon Dwyryd, transporting slate down to the sea for export. Women often gathered cockles in the estuary, which they sold in local markets.

Prior to the middle of the 19th century, the area which is now the centre of the village, where there is now a good little shopping centre, was a large stagnant pool surrounded by swamp. It was drained in 1852 and developed by land owner David Williams of Deudraeth Castle, who laid out the town in a similar fashion to Tremadog, with wide streets and open spaces.

The main manufacturing industry in Penrhyndeudraeth was established in 1872 to make guncotton. Cookes Explosives Ltd, dealing with increased demand for munitions during WW1, set up a new explosives manufacturing facility, bringing an economic boom to the town. The plant produced thousands of tons of munitions for the war and explosives for quarrying and mining. In 1949, R. T. Cooke applied for a licence to store explosives at Croesor Quarry. Many lost their lives during accidents at the works; a slate plaque has been erected on site to remember them and all who worked there. The prolonged miners' strike of 1984/5 and the competition from foreign coal imports resulted in wholesale pit closures which, in turn, reduced the demand for mining explosives to the point where production was no longer economic and the site was finally cleared in 1997. It is now a nature reserve.

Damien Hughes

'Earl of Merioneth' *heads through the verdant Vale of Ffestiniog, May 2014.*

'Taliesin' *on the 62' high Cei Mawr, March 2008.*

Above Rhiw Goch the line turns sharply to the right and runs across a dry-stone embankment, sixty feet high, known as Cei Mawr. If you look to the right here there is a wonderful view of the Afon Dwyryd and the Irish Sea with Harlech castle in the distance. The train plunges back into the woodland, with glimpses of rhododendrons, larch trees and the ancient sessile oaks of primeval Wales. Buzzards swirl lazily overhead and other creatures keep a watchful eye, unseen by the interloping humans.

After around a mile, a large house appears through the trees, situated a hundred feet or so below the railway on the right. This is Plas Tan y Bwlch, once the home of the Oakeley family, owners of one of the largest slate quarries in Blaenau Ffestiniog, now a Study Centre for the Snowdonia National Park Authority. Then, suddenly, a vista opens out to give a magnificent view of the village of Maentwrog and far-reaching views of the Vale of Ffestiniog. The train takes a sharp turn left and plunges into a deep curved rock cutting; Tyler's Curve. Just beyond, hidden in the woods, is the little station of Plas Halt. This request stop was built in the 1960s to serve Plas Tan y Bwlch.

Top: 'Merddin Emrys' *hurries through the trees of Coed Bryn Mawr, October 2010.*

Below: 'Blanche' *runs along a hillside ledge above the Dwyryd Valley, September 2009.*

Cei Mawr

Cei Mawr is one of the most impressive structures along the line. It is a tall, curved, dry-stone embankment that stands some 62 feet above the level of the stream below.

Since construction numerous repairs have been required and the present structure is significantly wider than the original. Between 1887 and 1890 nearly a thousand pounds was spent on strengthening work, including building buttresses on the north east side and the south eastern end.

In earlier days sidings existed at both ends, to the north for Bwlch-y-Plwm lead mine and at the south for Catherine and Jane Lead Mining Company Ltd.

In early 2008, with the aid of outside agencies, the views around the Cei Mawr area were greatly improved. The FR aided the removal of felled trees from the area.

Tyler's Curve

This is the sharpest curve on the line, where up trains change direction from North East to North West around the hanging valley of Llyn Mair. Passengers on the valley side have a good view of Maentwrog village and the Vale of Ffestiniog. Having a radius of only 2½ chains, it is the tightest on the operational railway. It is named after Captain Tyler, the Inspecting Officer appointed by the Board of Trade who recommended approval of the FR's application to open the line to public passenger traffic. This whole section of line would have been by-passed by tunnels if the proposed 1869 double tracking had gone ahead.

Plas Tan y Bwlch

Plas Tan y Bwlch is the Snowdonia National Park Authority's Environmental Studies Centre. The Centre aims to provide courses which are of interest to all lovers of the countryside who would like to learn more about this fascinating part of Wales.

Accommodation is provided in a well-appointed country house which for many years was the Welsh home of the Oakeley family, important quarry and land owners in the area. The carefully tended gardens and the well-engineered steps and paths are worth exploring, as you will find rare trees and shrubs throughout the 100-acre estate.

Maentwrog

This small community was built as an estate village by the Oakeley family, and riverside walks lead from the village following a meander of the Afon Dwyryd. The meander is not a natural feature, it was created by the estate owners in the 1800s to give a more visually appealing view from their house.

In the churchyard, standing next to the porch, is a stone of unknown origin. According to legend, pagan rites being held on the land where the church now stands disgusted a giant called Twrog. After watching from a nearby hill he threw a large stone, which hit the altar the pagans were using and destroyed it. His thumb and finger mark can still be seen in the rock. Afterwards Twrog settled in the area and his followers erected a church where the boulder was embedded in the ground.

Another explanation is that Twrog was the early Celtic Christian who founded the first church here, and that he stood on the stone to preach.

The Grapes Hotel is a 17th century coaching inn, although an ancient cellar is known to date back to the 13th century. This Grade II Listed building, is chronicled in George Borrow's book Wild Wales where he entered ... "a magnificent parlour and partook of Brandy and water". Other famous visitors from the past include the great statesman Lloyd George and Lilley Langtry who "took tea".

Above: *The buffet steward looks out at Plas Halt while the train makes a brief stop. The carriage in the foreground is No.14, which was originally from the Lynton & Barnstaple Railway in North Devon.*

Below: *Tranquil Plas Halt is connected by various woodland paths to the Snowdonia National Park study centre at Plas Tan y Bwlch.*

Roger Dimmick

Above: 'Palmerston' *and* 'Taliesin' *arrive at Tan y Bwlch station on their way to Blaenau Ffestiniog, while* 'Blanche' *waits to depart with a train to Porthmadog, March 2009.*

The railway now sweeps round in a great curve, round a hanging valley, towards Tan y Bwlch station. If you look across the valley, you can sometimes glimpse, through the trees, another train heading in the same direction. This is a Porthmadog bound train coming towards you! You will meet it at Tan y Bwlch station, situated above the beautiful Llyn Mair, some two miles from the main road in the valley.

At Tan y Bwlch the train will sometimes stop for a short time, waiting for another train to arrive in the passing loop. The peace is then disrupted by a rush of activity as people change trains or hurry across the footbridge to the station café. As your train departs, look out to the right where there is a view of Llyn Mair below you. The lake was given to Mary Oakeley, one of the daughters of the 'big house' in the 19th century, as a 21st birthday present, hence the name.

Set in the beautiful Snowdonia National Park, Tan y Bwlch station is an excellent place to break your journey. There are nature trails to follow through the forest, lakes and streams to investigate, and a wide variety of wildlife. The station café serves a wide selection of hot and cold food and is licensed, so you can if you wish slake your thirst with a selection of bottled beers.

At certain times of the year jazz trains run to Tan y Bwlch. On these occasions you can enjoy food from the barbeque while listening to a foot-stomping live jazz band. These trains are very popular, so make sure you book well in advance.

Tan y Bwlch café is also available for private hire. It has a licence to perform weddings or, if you wish, you can book the venue for a private party. Please phone our main Booking Office - 01766 516024 - for more information.

Roy Woods

Llyn Mair

Llyn Mair (Mary's Lake) was artificially created as a 21st birthday present for W.E.Oakeley's daughter, Mary (Mair in Welsh).

The lake is actually the lowest in its own little system. From one source on the flanks of Moelwyn Bach, a stream passes through both Llyn y Garnedd Uchaf and Llyn y Garnedd Isaf, passing beneath the FR at Creuau Bank, before reaching Llyn Mair itself. From the valley leading towards Rhyd a stream flows through Llyn Hafod y Llyn (another artificial lake) under the FR and on to Llyn Mair.

From its dammed eastern end Llyn Mair's outflow becomes a tributary of Afon Dwyryd, which George Borrow (in his book "Wild Wales") calls the Tan y Bwlch river.

Today the lake has a walk around it and has a popular picnic area.

THE GARDENS AT PLAS TAN Y BWLCH

Discover the beautiful gardens and grounds of Plas Tan y Bwlch, a spectacular Victorian garden nestling in dramatic mountain scenery within the Snowdonia National Park. Covering 13 acres, this 'garden for all seasons' hosts a magnificent collection of flowering rhododendrons and azaleas in spring which includes a 120-year-old rhododendron tunnel. In summer, shrubs, roses and herbaceous plants growing in the warm south-facing sunny borders are a delight and in October and early November the autumn leaf-colours are not to be missed.

Overlooking the garden is a dramatic Victorian-Gothic mansion, which was once home to wealthy slate-quarry-owners the Oakeley family. Now run as the Snowdonia National Park Authority's study centre, it is also possible for garden visitors to view inside this historic building.

Much of the Plas gardens seen today were originally laid out for William Edward Oakeley by Head Gardener John Roberts in a period lasting from 1879 until 1912. This garden post-dates earlier landscapes works which were carried out on the estate in the romantic picturesque-style very much in favour during the 18th and early 19th centuries. These earlier works, commissioned by William Edward Oakeley's grandfather William Oakeley, included improving the agricultural land in the valley, which until his arrival was a tidal estuary (today the actual coastline is two miles away). He built nearly a mile of embankments to contain the river and reclaimed the land from regular flooding. It is also suggested that he altered the river's course and created a series of graceful meanderings to enhance the aesthetic nature of the view from the mansion above.

During the winter of 2013 – 2014 North West Wales was battered by a succession of terrible storms culminating in the 'St Valentine's Day Storm' which subjected Plas Tan y Bwlch to wind speeds in excess of 103mph on the 13th and 14th February 2014. Visitors in 2016 will have the opportunity to view parts of the garden undergoing a fascinating restoration following extensive damage during those storms.

Visitors can also enjoy Plas Tan y Bwlch's Victorian conservatory tea room with its stunning views across the Maentwrog valley, a video presentation on the history of this astonishing estate and follow estate walks which lead past the beautiful waters of Llyn Mair to Tan y Bwlch station, where the Ffestiniog Railway can be joined.

The Oakelys

The Oakeleys were influential in the creation of the Ffestiniog Railway, which dramatically increased the amount of dressed slate that could be transported from the Blaenau quarries to the waiting ships at Porthmadog. William Griffith Oakeley worked with the Ffestiniog Railway Company to establish the route which crossed Plas Tan y Bwlch land immediately above the mansion. On February 26th 1833, Oakeley was granted the honour of laying the first stone of the railway construction at Creuau, which is close to Tan y Bwlch station.

Canolfan Parc Cenedlaethol Eryri
Snowdonia National Park Centre

PLAS TAN Y BWLCH

Canolfan Parc Cenedlaethol Eryri /
Snowdonia National Park Centre

Plas Tan y Bwlch, Maentwrog,
Blaenau Ffestinog, LL41 3YU

Ffón / Tel: 01766 772600

Roger Dimmick

Above: *The oldest working steam locomotive in regular service in the world, 'Prince', takes water at Tan y Bwlch.*

Coed y Bleiddiau and the Willow Wolf

Local legend says here was home to the last wolf in Wales, hence the name Coed y Bleiddiau. Wolves became extinct in England in the early 1600s but lived on in the wilds of Wales for much longer. They were probably still around during the Civil War – there is talk of a Knight's grave nearby, maybe he slew the last wolf? Or was he a victim?

This wolf has every chance of living forever, as a vigorous type of willow (salix viminalis) was planted in March 2010. The wolf was designed and built by Beryl Smith of Llanidloes and funded by the Countryside Council for Wales (CCW).

The skimpy fence is there to give the willow a sporting chance against the ravenous wild goats which come and go as they please. Once the willow gets established the fence will come down and children will be able to crawl into the belly and exit by the tail which doubles as a tunnel.

A few minutes after leaving Tan y Bwlch we slow down to negotiate the short, but very restricted, Garnedd tunnel, which is only just wide enough for the train, and is a stark reminder never to poke your head out of the window when travelling on the Ffestiniog Railway. Once clear of the tunnel the train proceeds through the woodland with a view south towards Trawsfynydd and its now-redundant nuclear power station. After a short distance we pass, on the left, a bungalow called Coed y Bleiddiau, or 'Wood of the Wolves'. Sadly there are no longer any real wolves in the wood! However, if you look out to the valley side of the train, an impressive "willow wolf" reminds the traveller of what used to be. The cottage here was originally built as a Permanent Way Inspector's House. It is not known for how long it fulfilled this function. However, for many decades the Company let it to a succession of tenants, including Sir Granville Bantock, the British Musician and Composer, who came to prominence towards the end of the 19th century, and whose career lasted well into the 1930s. The cottage is now in the care of the Landmark Trust. When they have completed its full restoration, it will become a holiday let. It has no road access, so sometimes the train has to stop to make a delivery, or pick up a passenger.

Beyond a sweeping right hand curve (a good place for photographs of the engine from the back of the train!) there is a tiny halt with the intriguing name of Campbell's Platform. This was originally a private station for the use of Colonel Campbell, a solicitor, builder and licensed shot firer who lived in Dduallt Manor, the big house which can be seen just below the railway. Colonel Campbell did much of the blasting needed on the deviation line above Dduallt in the 1960s and '70s. There is a memorial to him on Dduallt Station.

20

Roger Dimmick

Passing under a bridge, the train enters Dduallt station, with the deserted house, Rhoslyn, next to the line. The railway crosses over itself at Dduallt, going round in a spiral, the only one in Britain. In the late 1950s the route of the old railway north from Dduallt was blocked by the construction of the Tanygrisiau pumped-storage power station and Llyn Ystradau reservoir, which drowned the trackbed. The solution adopted was to build an alternative route – the deviation – to the west of the reservoir, with the Dduallt spiral being constructed to raise the level of the line. Keep an eye out for a herd of feral mountain goats who live hereabouts, descendants from medieval farming, now running wild amongst the trees.

From Dduallt there is a particularly attractive walk along the old trackbed from the northern end of the platform, which takes you over the original railway tunnel and alongside the lake. You should come out across the dam at Llyn Ystradau and end up at Tanygrisiau station.

Huw Jenkins

Top: 'David Lloyd George' *on the curve at Campbell's Platform, August 2006.*

Below: *The old trackbed can be clearly seen beyond the platform at Dduallt.*

Roger Dimmick

Plas y Dduallt

Plas y Dduallt (House on the Black Hillside) built in the 1560s with the front extension added in 1605, was home to the Lloyds, minor nobles with a link to Llywelyn the Great. By the 1960s the house was close to ruin when Colonel Campbell bought and restored it. The Colonel allowed the 'deviationists' rebuilding the line to Blaenau to stay in the farm buildings and these were known as Dduallt Mess. In return he got Campbell's Platform with the right to run his own engine aptly called 'The Colonel'. *The Mess, which used to sleep seventeen in bunk beds, is now a characterful holiday cottage for four. More information on the house, the cottage and its intriguing history can be found at* **www.campbellscottage.co.uk**

Roger Dimmick

Gwilym Deudraeth, the Ffestiniog Railway Poet

During the 1880s, the Railway employed a young man, William Edwards, as stationmaster at Dduallt. William was the son of a sea captain and was born in Penrhyndeudraeth. Unfortunately, although he received a good basic education, he does not appear to have been overly fond of hard work and tried his hand at various things, including working in one of the quarries in Blaenau Ffestiniog. There he met men who delighted in the cynghanedd, a type of poetry originating in the Middle Ages which still flourishes today. He quickly took to the art and could turn out englynion - strict-metre verses - which delighted his fellow workers.

The post of stationmaster at Dduallt (Rhosllyn as it was then called) became vacant and seemed to William to be the ideal job; not hard work, plenty of time to watch nature and compose englynion. The voice of the ordinary railway worker is not often heard, but Gwilym Deudraeth gives us some glimpses of the camaraderie and monotony of a railwayman's life. He has left us many poems about his time on the railway and the scenery and nature he saw around him.

The train, however, turns sharply right and climbs steeply, passing over the bridge you've just come under and runs parallel with the old route, but higher up the hillside, past the derelict cottage of Gelliwiog on the left. The train then burrows into the mountain in a new tunnel constructed in the 1970s, through the wall of an old dam, threading its way along the side of Llyn Ystradau towards the Ffestiniog Power Station. See if you can work out where the old railway crossed the lake – but note that you can only see this at 'low tide'! Behind the power station the train crosses over the massive penstock pipes which feed water to the turbines on a bridge buried below the tracks.

Top: 'Linda' *climbs round the spiral at Dduallt, with the houses of Llan Ffestiniog visible across the valley.*

Below: *The old trackbed can be seen from the right hand side of the train; this drystone wall carried the track towards the old Moelwyn tunnel.*

Catalin Mubteanu

This is the summit of the line. Because of 'the Deviation', the track is no longer on its original ruling gradient. When the original gravity trains are re-created at Gala events, they now have to be released from here, behind the power station. Blaenau Ffestiniog and its immediate environs are situated in an 'island' not included in the Snowdonia National Park. A sign on the ground on the run down to Valvehouse road crossing marks the boundary. On the left can be seen the incline reaching up to a tunnel in the mountain, leading to Wrysgan Quarry.

Top: *'Merddin Emrys' heads past the power station and Llyn Ystradau, August 2010.*

Below: *The valley and old railway routes as they looked in 1956.*

Pumped storage hydro-electricity

This is a method of storing electricity for use during periods of high demand. At times of low demand, excess electricity is used to pump water into an elevated reservoir. When there is high demand, water is released back into the lower reservoir through a turbine, generating hydroelectricity. About 70% of the energy used to pump water into the upper reservoir can be regained in this process.

Llyn Stwlan, the upper reservoir of the Ffestiniog Pumped Storage Scheme, is several hundred feet above the railway. The power station has four reversible turbine-driven generators which can generate 360 MW of electricity within 60 seconds of the need arising, and which also act as motors to drive the pumps which return water to the upper reservoir.

This system is economical as it flattens out the variations in the load on the power grid, permitting installations such as gas-fired and nuclear power stations that provide base-load electricity to continue operating at full capacity and reduces the need to build power plants which run only at peak times.

The scheme was completed in 1963. The upper reservoir was formed by enlarging Llyn Stwlan with a concrete dam 380m long and 34m high, the lower by damming the Afon Ystradau, with the power station built on its western side.

Bob Bloxworth

After crossing the Cwmorthin road, there is a picnic area on the right between the railway and the lake with an excellent café. The line crosses the Afon Cwmorthin on a bridge, with a spectacular waterfall on the left, just before the train enters Tanygrisiau station. Another token is taken from the signalbox; although this is technically a request stop, most trains stop here. This is where the old trackbed is regained and the Deviation is left behind. The old line is high above the village of Tanygrisiau and the old school, chapel and post office can be seen below.

Top: 'Merddin Emrys' *approaching Tanygrisiau with a long train, September 2009.*

Left: *Afon Cwmorthin.*

Below: *Lakeside café sits in a delightful spot close to Tanygrisiau station. The trains pass behind while the lake sits to the front. It is a great place for starting or finishing a walk or just to sit and watch the world go by.*

Roy Woods

Clare Britton

24

Roger Dimmick

Above: *Passengers relax in the First Class carriage, as 'David Lloyd George' climbs out of Tanygrisiau station so it can pass behind the power station, September 2007.*

Below: *Above the rooftops; the view from a Porthmadog-bound train approaching Tanygrisiau, August 2012.*

Roy Woods

As the line twists and turns, passing very close to cottages, the industrial nature of Blaenau Ffestiniog becomes apparent with the sight of many old inclines which used to link the various quarries with the railway.

Just before Glan y Pwll is Dinas Junction, although little trace of it can be seen now. Originally the old line used to go straight on here to Dinas, but its course is largely covered by slate waste. A new alignment was built in 1899

Top: 'Blanche' *and* 'Prince' *on the ledge above Tanygrisiau. The snow-covered Moelwyns form a backdrop showing the extent of the quarry inclines at the top of the line.*

Below: 'Lilla' *shunts the Alco* 'Mountaineer' *on the old Dinas branch, outside Glan y Pwll works, with the Afon Barlwyd in the foreground, October 2012.*

Pant yr Afon

At the end of the old branch to Dinas was Rhiwbryfdir, although the site of the village is now entirely obliterated by the quarry tippings. It was the original terminating point of the FR in 1836. At Rhiwbryfdir, there was a magnificent viaduct spanning the Afon Barlwyd, the road and both the FR line and the standard gauge Conwy Valley line. The Welsh Slate Co., taken over by W.E. Oakeley in the early 1880s, built the viaduct in an attempt to find more land for the dumping of slate waste. This became the Glan-y-don tip. The right hand support column can still be seen today. Sadly, little remains of this viaduct now.

26

Above: *A busy day at Blaenau Ffestiniog with all platforms in use. Arriva Trains Wales' premier service train, 'Y Gerallt Gymro (Gerald of Wales)'* sits in the loop line whilst on a private charter. (Chris Parry)

to allow further encroachment by the huge slate tip to the left of the railway. The new alignment is more or less on the track following the river, next to Glan y Pwll sidings. The current railway follows the trackbed of what was originally the Duffws branch, as the main line served many quarries towards Rhiwbryfdir.

The train crosses the Afon Barlwyd and the railway's permanent way depot at Glan y Pwll is on the left. The train whistles for the level crossing and curves round to the right past the old (now demolished) London & North Western Railway station. As the train nears Blaenau Ffestiniog, the town's elegant Market Hall is on the left. There have been several plans over the last few years to turn the building into a centre for the arts, although so far without success. There is a sharp climb here passing under the Dorvil Road bridge, past St David's church, on the approach to Blaenau Ffestiniog station. The station is shared with National Rail services and is situated on the site of the old Great Western station, originally the terminus of the branch line from Bala. The new joint station was opened in 1982.

Blaenau Ffestiniog is the largest town in old Merionethshire. Although not included in the borders of the Snowdonia National Park it has much to commend it as a centre to explore the area. Not only is it connected to the coast of Cardigan Bay by means of the Ffestiniog Railway, there is also the beautiful Conwy Valley line which offers the traveller an easy way to reach Betws y Coed, Llanwrst and Llandudno. Where possible, the narrow gauge trains are timed to allow a change of trains to be made with those going to and from the North Wales coast. From Llandudno Junction, there are trains to Bangor and Holyhead, as well as Colwyn Bay, Rhyl, Chester, Shrewsbury, Crewe and Manchester.

The Conwy Valley Line

The Conwy Valley line train takes you from the slate mining town of Blaenau Ffestiniog to the beautiful bay of "the Queen of the Welsh Resorts" at Llandudno on a 30 mile journey of contrasts along the Lledr and Conwy valleys. The scenery changes from the rugged mountains and splendour of the Snowdonia National Park to the gentle rolling pastures at sea level. The train descends from 790 feet above sea level passing through the mountains to arrive at the Victorian seaside town of Llandudno.

Above: *The evening sun illuminates a vintage train crossing The Cob.* (Chris Parry)

Below: *Replica Manning Wardle Lynton & Barnstable locomotive 'Lyd', built at the FR's Boston Lodge works, rests a while at Minffordd with a train for Porthmadog, August 2012.* (Roy Woods)

Roger Dimmick

Roy Woods

As this was a success, he turned his attention to Tremadog, in 1806 merely an area of marshland in the Glaslyn Estuary; he was responsible for its reclamation. The town was built as Madocks envisaged - the last staging post on the London-Ireland stage coach route, via the anticipated new harbour at Porth Dinllaen on the Llŷn peninsula. At that time the Menai Straits and the Afon Conwy were not bridged.

Encouraged by his achievements, Madocks' next great success was the reclamation of the wide Glaslyn estuary, building an embankment, locally known as the Cob, between 1808 and 1811. This diverted the Afon Glaslyn which created a new harbour between 1821 and 1825: hence the town's name which translates as "Madog's Port". However, many local people believe the name celebrates the fabled voyage of Prince Madog to America in the tenth century AD. It can be regarded as celebrating both.

Several shipyards were built on the quayside and these were to bring prosperity to the little town. In the 1870s it was estimated that over a thousand vessels used the harbour in any one year, and, at its peak in 1873, over 116,000 tons of Blaenau slate left Porthmadog for all parts of the world.

Purple Moose Brewery
Bragdy Mŵs Piws

Purple Moose Brewery has produced beer in Porthmadog since June 2005, creating quality local ales for the discerning drinkers of North-West Wales.

Purple Moose Brewery has been awarded many accolades for its range of beers including two times Regional Champion and Champion Beer of Wales, as well as awards at national level.

Local Produce Market

On the last Saturday of each month, there is a Local Produce Market at Y Ganolfan, next to the Harbour. It's open from 9.00am to 2.00pm.

Kerfoots

Kerfoots award-winning department store is well worth a visit. The wonderful atmosphere within the delightful Victorian building is enhanced by the unique spiral staircase, chandeliers and the slender cast iron columns which support the upper floors. It also houses Porthmadog's own Millennium Dome, constructed in 1999 by local craftsmen to celebrate the store's 125th anniversary. Made of stained glass, it depicts how Porthmadog looked in 1874.

Andrew Kime www.imagesofsnowdonia.com

Roger Dimmick

Shipbuilding

Before the construction of the Cob, ships had been built at a number of locations around Traeth Mawr. As the town developed, a number of the shipbuilders from the Meirionnydd side moved to the new port, building brigs, schooners, barquentines and brigantines. After the arrival of the railway in 1867 there was a drop off in trade but the shipbuilders, owners, brokers and the seamen themselves fought back and found new trades. A new type of ship was developed with one trade in mind - the Newfoundland and Labrador salt cod industry. These were the "Western Ocean Yachts" for which Porthmadog is justly famous. Thirty two of these fine ships were built at Porthmadog between 1891 and 1913. In all, over 260 ships were built at Porthmadog and Borth y Gest between 1825 until shipbuilding came to an end in 1913.

During the 1970s, a private maritime museum was established in an old ketch, the 'Garlandstone', built in Devon in 1908. The museum collected a range of material relating to the port and its ships. The museum became part of Gwynedd Maritime Museum, and is now Porthmadog Maritime Museum. The 'Garlandstone' passed to the National Museums & Galleries of Wales. In 1987, the ship was leased to Morwellham Quay Industrial Museum, Devon, and in 2000 became its property.

Gwynedd Archives

1832b. Portmadoc Harbour, in Olden

Above: *Portmadoc Harbour, seen from Ynys Tywyn.*

Martin Pritchard collection

'Gestiana'

The three-mast schooner 'Gestiana' was built by David Williams of Porthmadog in 1913. She was the last ship to be built at Porthmadog. This photograph was taken on the occasion of her official launch from David Williams' yard. It is worth noting that the christening bottle failed to break at the first attempt - a sign which did not bode well for the future, as she sank in October 1913 on her maiden voyage.

The three-masted ships that carried the slate from Porthmadog were also built around Tremadog Bay and in the four shipyards by the delightful little bay at Borth y Gest. Today, this is still a favourite place for those who love the sea more than simply lying on the beach.

Porthmadog expanded rapidly as a slate exporting port. Welsh slate was in high demand as a construction material in the English industrial cities and abroad, and was transported to the new port by horse drawn tramways. By 1873 116,000 tons (117,800 t) of slate were being shipped out of Porthmadog, and other trade was being developed. The Carnarvonshire and Merionethshire Steamship Company had been formed in 1864 and purchased the '*Rebecca*' to carry stores from Liverpool to supply the growing town.

In the 19th century Porthmadog had at least three iron foundries. The Glaslyn Foundry was opened in 1848, and the Union Iron Works in 1869. The Britannia Foundry, opposite Porthmadog Harbour Railway Station, was established in 1851 and grew rapidly as the town's prosperity increased. The business produced slate working machinery and railway equipment, supplying goods to all but one of the slate quarries operating in England and Wales. A lucrative sideline was the production of large numbers of drains and manhole covers for Caernarfonshire's roads.

The First World War marked the end of Porthmadog's export trade. No new ships were built, several were sunk by enemy action, and most of the surviving fleet was sold. The arrival of the LNWR, in 1879, and the GWR, in 1883, at Blaenau Ffestiniog was responsible for the steady decline in the slate traffic carried by the Ffestiniog Railway and by Porthmadog shipping. Some slate had been carried via the Ffestiniog Railway, the Croesor & Portmadoc Railway and the Cambrian Railways after the latter's line had been opened between Barmouth and Pwllheli in 1867; this traffic was diverted to the exchange yard established between the Ffestiniog Railway and the Cambrian Railways at Minffordd in 1872. By 1925 less than five percent of Ffestiniog's slate output went out by sea. The final load of slate, delivered by rail, left by sea from Porthmadog in 1946 and two months later the railway ceased commercial operations.

Rob Piercy Gallery

Established in 1986, the Rob Piercy Gallery is an artist run gallery situated close to the centre of Porthmadog. The gallery has four exhibiting spaces, surrounding a quiet courtyard. The building was converted into an art gallery in 1986 having previously been an old water board warehouse.

The gallery features a large selection of Rob Piercy watercolours, limited edition and open edition prints as well as a large selection of greeting cards of his work. There is also a fine display of unique craftwork and jewellery.

Pen Cei was the centre of the harbour's commercial activities. Boats were built and repaired and there were slate wharves for each quarry company, with tracks connecting to the railway. Bron Guallt, built in 1895, was the Oakeley Quarry shipping agent's house. Y Grisiau Mawr (The Great Stairs) connected the quay to Garth and the houses built to house the ship owners and sea captains, and it was here that the School of Navigation was built.

The Royal Sportsman Hotel (Gwesty'r Heliwr) on Y Stryd Fawr (the High Street) was built in 1862 to be a staging post on the turnpike road to Porthdinllaen. The arrival of the railway five years later brought increasing numbers of tourists, and the hotel soon became famous for its liveried carriage and horses, which transported guests to local sightseeing spots. The building was constructed using Ffestiniog slate, and the original stone and slate fireplaces are still in position.

There are many places to eat in Porthmadog, including two curry houses, numerous cafés, two Chinese take-aways and Allports fish and chip shop. Don't forget Spooner's café and bar at Harbour Station……..

Black Rock Sands

One of the very few beaches in Britain where you can step out of the car and straight on to the sands, which stretch as far as you can see. The surrounding sand dunes have been designated a Site of Special Scientific Interest, affording spectacular views of all Cardigan Bay.

Sunbathe and swim to your heart's content whilst enjoying mountain scenery. The shallow water makes it a haven for youngsters, but note that the area is popular with jet ski and powerboat enthusiasts. These are kept well away from sensible bathers. Facilities include beach parking, toilets, showers, drinking water, dog and craft restriction zones and a launch area.

Above and Below: *Porthmadog, a town full of contrasts - with a bustling high street, but many quiet lanes to explore as well.*

PORTMEIRION

Portmeirion

This unique village is set in its own private grounds, about two miles walk from Minffordd station. It was created by self-trained Welsh architect Sir Clough Williams-Ellis (1883-1978) to demonstrate how a naturally beautiful place could be developed without spoiling it. Portmeirion is made up of about 50 buildings, parts for many of which were rescued from redevelopment schemes elsewhere in the UK, most of these buildings are also part of the hotel. There are just the right number of interesting shops, galleries, tea shops and restaurants to keep you amused and there are some beautiful coastal walks with stunning views, as the village is surrounded by 70 acres of sub-tropical woodland gardens. You'll be charmed by this truly romantic corner of Wales.

Just off the main driveway, about halfway from Minffordd, is Castell Deudraeth, a Victorian mansion recently restored as a restaurant and hotel, also part of the Portmeirion complex.

Not far from the railway, some two miles from Minffordd station, is the Italianate village of Portmeirion. Created by the architect Clough Williams Ellis in the early Twentieth Century, the village boasts some beautiful gardens with many outstanding specimen trees and shrubs. The village is famous for its location for Patrick MacGoohan's 1960s television series 'The Prisoner'. Be seeing you!

A pleasant walk of a couple of miles from Penrhyn station, at Llanfrothen, is Plas Brondanw. Leaving Penrhyn station, turn left and head uphill, cross the railway at the level crossing and keep on following the main road. The house was built in 1550 by John ap Hywel and is listed Grade II*. It has never been bought or sold and was for many years the home of Sir Clough Williams-Ellis. It is now owned by the Second Portmeirion Foundation. The gardens at Plas Brondanw are a fine example of Sir Clough's talent for creative landscape design. The main features date from the early part of the 20th century before he began Portmeirion, but work continued on and off until the 1960s. Inspired by the renaissance gardens of Italy, the design of the Plas gardens is strongly architectural, relying on stone wall, topiary and avenues of trees to form the vistas which lead the eye to distant mountain tops. The gardens are open to the public daily all year round.

TAN Y BWLCH

Roger Dimmick

Clare Britton

Tan y Bwlch café is a great excuse to break your journey.

Tan y Bwlch is the half way point on the railway. At roughly thirty minutes on the train from Porthmadog or from Blaenau Ffestiniog, it's great for families with younger children. There is a splendid new Play Area, just next to the Café, where the younger members of the family can play in safety. The woodland here is also a great adventure playground for children of all ages.

Our licensed Café serves hot and cold drinks, as well as meals, cakes and a range of tempting locally-sourced foods. Tan y Bwlch is a wonderful place for a picnic, or a delightful haven just to while away the time with a pot of tea, listening to the birdsong.

There are splendid views across the valley and some pleasant walks along the nature trails down to Llyn Mair. The more adventurous can strike out through the woodland paths towards Dduallt and even on to Tanygrisiau.

During August, there are barbecue and jazz evenings, although you'll need to book in advance for these evening trains as they are extremely popular. In the winter, Siôn Corn (Santa) has his special trains from Porthmadog and Blaenau Ffestiniog on the weekends leading up to Christmas. His elves can often be seen carrying the sack loads of presents for our smaller guests.

Roy Woods

While the engine takes water, a friendly buffet steward will tempt you with a copy of the Guide Book......or even ice cream in summer!

Top: *A quiet summer's morning at Tan y Bwlch before the first train of the day arrives.*
Below: *Summer's evening entertainment with freshly cooked food and live jazz music.*

Children's play area

2010 saw welcome improvements to the children's play area beside the café. The Ffestiniog Railway Society and the Friends of Tan y Bwlch have jointly sponsored new equipment and Astroturf, along with additional drainage.

Roger Dimmick

Jan Woods

BLAENAU FFESTINIOG

Slate Caverns for Recreation

A legacy of the slate industry is the large number of caverns inside the mountains that surround Blaenau Ffestiniog. Many are flooded or unsafe after years of neglect, but others are being turned into fascinating activity centres – underground.

Llechwedd Slate Caverns - Just outside Blaenau Ffestiniog on the A470, Llechwedd is one of the oldest mining attractions in the area. It's newly revamped Deep Mine Tour is the UK's only 'Enhanced Reality Deep Mine Experience'. Have a go at mining slate the Victorian way, set off an explosion, witness the aerial 'danger man' 100ft up in the air and learn how the slate was won - all 500ft underground.

Zip World Experience Adventure – These new attractions makes use of some of Llechwedd's other caverns. Bounce Below is a subterranean playground, installed with huge bouncy trampolines and slides. Zip World Caverns is a great offer for those adrenaline junkies with zip wires flying through the huge caverns. Zip World Titan at Llechwedd is the largest zip zone in Europe, allowing four riders to travel at once.

Go Below – This attraction operates from the station car park at Tanygrisiau and challenges you to test your nerve by journeying through a mountain via a series of exciting challenges on one of two epic underground adventures.

Note: pre-booking is required for most of these attractions, details of which can all be found via **www.blaenauffestiniog.org**

Top: *Blaenau Ffestiniog from Moelwyn Bach showing the large waste heaps that dominate the town, December 2005.*

Blaenau Ffestiniog is a relatively new town, created following the discovery of the valuable slate vein in the area in the 18th Century. But Ffestiniog parish itself goes back a few centuries. Many ancient remains can be seen dotted around the area, with sites dating back to the Bronze and Iron Ages, and there is also evidence of the Roman period.

Towards Cwm Cynfal, some of the place-names remind one of the magical stories recorded in the world famous folk tales, Y Mabinogi, where some of the tales are located. By following some of the footpaths a number of well-known valleys may be reached, Cwmorthin, Cwm Bowydd, Cwm Cynfal, Cwm Teigl, each with its own particular historical features – and superb views. Sarn Helen is a noted Roman road, which recalls the arrival of the Roman Legions to nearby Tomen-y-mur, a Roman camp, around the 2nd or 3rd Centuries AD.

Evidence can be seen all around the town of man's pursuit for a livelihood from the slate – and the slate waste is a reminder of the thriving industry in the area. According to tradition, it was late in the 1760s that one Methusalem Jones, from Arfon, dreamt of a location where the rock slabs split perfectly, and ventured to start a small business at a place that later became known as

40

Roger Dimmick

Roger Dimmick

Diffwys Quarry, in this town. Diffwys was soon followed by many other slate quarries. One of those quarries, the Oakeley, grew into what became the largest underground slate workings in the world, which has, unbelievably, around fifty miles of railway track in its various underground levels in the bowels of the surrounding mountains. Hence the beginning of a thriving industry which developed into one of the largest slate centres in the world. Out of a secluded part of Ffestiniog parish mushroomed a community that became the highest populated in all of Merionethshire and the second largest in the whole of North Wales by 1901.

At one time over 4000 men worked in the local slate quarries, which contributed greatly to the local economy. To improve transportation for the slate, the Ffestiniog Railway was opened in 1836, replacing the pack-mules and sailing ships on the Afon Dwyryd. Later two other railways, the LNWR (later LMS) and the GWR both built branch lines to Blaenau Ffestiniog to tap into this lucrative trade. Dôl Wen hydro power station was built to provide electricity for the local quarries in 1899, and in May 1902, Blaenau Ffestiniog became the first town in Britain to have its streets lit with electricity provided by the power of water.

Top: *St. David's Church, Blaenau Ffestiniog.*
Below: *Ty Gorsaf and the High Street, Blaenau Ffestiniog.*

Roy Woods

The word on the street: celebrating Blaenau's Heritage – Poetry Trail

Blaenau Ffestiniog has a dynamic history and unique cultural identity. From a wealth of original quarry terms to a host of poets, writers and musicians, Blaenau's creativity produced a priceless cultural heritage. To reflect this rich heritage, hundreds of local sayings, unique quarry terms, historical references, and quotations from local artists were chosen for inclusion on the slate bands that are seen on the town's streets. Also included are contemporary sayings, as well as phrases created in workshops held with pupils of the local schools, reflecting current cultural identity as well as the community's hopes and dreams for the future.

A celebration of Blaenau's colourful culture, the phrases have been numbered to encourage you to walk the town's high street as you learn of this vibrant and unique heritage.

If you're catching the bus from the Station, or looking over the Moelwynion from the viewing canopy, look down under your feet! In the bus stops you'll find paving inscribed with the names of different sizes of roofing slates, from Narrow Ladies to Wide Viscountesses; the names were usually based upon female aristocracy. In the viewing canopy you'll find a "zero" in the middle of a triangle; this was the format for mile markers on the Ffestiniog Railway, with "zero point" being the town centre where the slates started their journey across the world.

Roger Dimmick

Clare Britton

Antur 'Stiniog – Mountain Biking

Antur 'Stiniog is a not for profit social enterprise. It was set up to develop the potential of the Outdoor Sector in the Ffestiniog area in a sustainable and innovative way for the benefit of the local residents and economy. The company aims to realise this vision through a number of exciting projects which vary from enjoyment and training in the sector to running a series of Mountain bike trails in the area.

The downhill mountain biking centre is based at Llechwedd Slate Caverns and has been recognised as being of World class standard, having hosted several national championship rounds in recent years. It has five routes of differing ability with an uplift shuttle in operation giving the opportunity to do between 10 and 15 descents in a day. The downhill centre is open Thursday to Sunday all through the year. There is a shop, café and changing facilities on site. Booking is required and can be done via the website. www.anturstiniog.com

Antur 'Stiniog also operate a shop and information service in the town centre offering general tourist information about what's on in town and the local area as well as having detailed knowledge of activities on offer. There is electric cycle hire available too. This is a great place to start your Blaenau experience to find out what is going on.

Roger Dimmick

Above: *These four pillars represent slate splitting chisels.*

Roger Dimmick

An imaginative £4.5m scheme to regenerate the town was undertaken in 2012, seeking to celebrate the wealth of heritage but also looking to a new future. The vision is to: "Create an exciting, vibrant and attractive place to live, work and visit, renowned for culture and the arts, our strong sense of community and the stunning environment. The town will build on these unique characteristics in a sustainable manner in order to achieve economic, social and environmental regeneration."

Antur 'Stiniog

Roger Dimmick

Roger Dimmick

Roger Dimmick

Above: *Blaenau Ffestiniog - a town worth exploring!*

Places to eat

There are several small cafés and eating places in Blaenau Ffestiniog, many of which are just a short walk from the station. From home made cakes and freshly brewed coffee at Isallt to larger meals in Bridge Café or DeNiros. There are takeaways too, including a great fish and chip restaurant and also a number of public houses. If you are travelling by car, you may want to venture further afield to the community run Pengwern Arms in Llan Ffestiniog or the Elen's Castle Hotel in nearby Dolwyddelan.

The old magistrates' court has been converted into an arts and music venue, with restaurant and bar, called CellB. There is also a recording studio, rehearsal space and a cinema.

Buried treasure

During the Second World War a different use was made of some of the slate caverns and this operation was carried out in total secrecy. Due to the dangers of enemy bombing over London, it was decided to transfer all of the art treasures at the National Gallery and from Buckingham Palace to Manod Quarry in 1941. Amongst the paintings stored there were works by Rubens, Rembrandt and Michelangelo. There were rumours at the time that the Crown Jewels were also stored there.......

From high level to low level Ffestiniog offers all kinds of walking. From Moelwyn Bach in the south to the high peak of Moel Siabod there is over 90 square kilometres of wild country to explore. To the south of Blaenau and towering above it are the Manods. Although the north peak of Manod Mawr is heavily quarried, the south peak is relatively untouched and wild. Its smaller brother, Manod Bach, is wild and untouched by paths. Nestling between the peaks is the beautiful Llyn Manod, ideal for a picnic.

For those not into high tops or wilderness areas, look for the village and woodland walks, such as Cwm Bowydd. Cynfal, on the edge of Llan Ffestiniog, which is breathtaking for its waterfalls. Or walk through the Maentwrog woods where old ancient oaks dominate and woodpeckers can be heard and seen. It is also the haunt of bats. These walks are described more fully in the excellent Blaenau Ffestiniog town guide (pictured here).

Blaenau Ffestiniog

diwylliant arbennig...
tirlun gwych
unique culture...
magnificent setting

www.blaenauffestiniog.org

NOTABLE PEOPLE OF BLAENAU FFESTINIOG

Ash Dome
Maentwrog N. Wales

David Nash -2000-

Above and Below: David Nash *'Ash Dome'*

Blaenau Ffestiniog Circle

Richard Long, one of the best-known British artists, spent two days collecting slate from Llechwedd Quarry for his brand new installation Blaenau Ffestiniog Circle (2011).

This work is a classic example of a Richard Long stone circle and embodies many of the central themes in his work expressing a powerful artistic engagement with landscape.

It was designed and built specifically for the National Museum Wales, following a lengthy period of collaboration in early 2011 and used Welsh slate collected directly by the artist at the Llechwedd Slate Mine in Blaenau Ffestiniog. With the support of the Art Fund, it is now set to remain at the National Museum Wales, where it will perform many roles and tell many different stories: the history of British sculpture, the centrality of landscape as subject in the visual arts, the history of conceptual strategies in art; and, not least, the way in which Wales continues to provide inspiration for internationally important artists working today.

David Nash, OBE RA (born 14 November 1945) is a British sculptor based in Blaenau Ffestiniog. Nash has worked worldwide with wood, trees and the natural environment. David Nash is known for works in wood and shaping living trees. His large wood sculptures are sometimes carved or partially burned to produce blackening. His main tools for these sculptures are a chainsaw and an axe to carve the wood and a blowtorch to char the wood.

Nash also makes land art, of which the best known is Wooden Boulder, begun in 1978. This work involves the journey of a large wooden sphere from a Welsh mountainside to the Atlantic Ocean. Over the years, the boulder has slipped, rolled and sometime been pushed through the landscape following the course of streams and rivers until finally it was last seen in the estuary of the Afon Dwyryd. It was thought to have been washed out to sea but, after being missing for over five years, the boulder reappeared in June 2009. Indications are that it had been buried in sand in the estuary. The sculptor had no idea of its location, and enjoys the notion that wood which grew out of the land will finally return to it.

Nash also makes sculptures which stay in the landscape. For example, Ash Dome is a ring of ash trees he planted in 1977 and trained to form a domed shape. The dome is sited at a secret location near Blaenau Ffestiniog and whenever it's filmed, crews are taken there by a circuitous route to guard its security.

Howard Bowcott (born 1956) is based in Penrhyndeudraeth and works on arts and regeneration projects throughout the UK and further afield. Over the last twenty five years he has developed a substantial reputation in the field of public art, as both designer and hands-on sculptor.

Bowcott's tribute to the slate industry of Wales, and the quarrymen who were and still are the driving force behind it, provides a fitting centrepiece to the Blaenau Ffestiniog regeneration project. The eye-catching work features a river motif, symbolising the ancient geological forces which created slate over 400 million years ago. It also references the nearby Afon Dwyryd, along which slates were transported to the coast before the Ffestiniog Railway was built.

Blaenau Ffestiniog poet Gwyn Thomas has created poetry especially for the slate river, including "Men die; the rocks in the empty darkness of these mountains endure."

Either side of the river the names of over 360 slate quarries have been engraved by Alan Hicks of Llechan Las, Blaenau Ffestiniog, featuring the many colours of slate from all over Wales. Each name is on a different coloured slate, corresponding to the shade produced by that quarry.

Falcon Hildred was born in Grimsby in 1935 and from the very beginning he was fascinated by the sounds, shapes and smells of industry. He came to know other working towns - mill towns and mining towns - and he liked the way they were so open about what they did. The cranes and viaducts, terrace-houses and lines of washing, dialects and factory sirens, gave them integrity and identity, and a vitality which has now been lost. A wartime move to Coventry extended his interest, and it was here at the age of thirteen that he began his art training, which he completed at the Royal College of Art, where he received a medal for work of distinction. Although an industrial designer by profession, he has spent most of his life recording industrial archaeology, under the theme title of Worktown. In 1993 he was made an honorary member of The Royal Society of Architects in Wales for "his consummate contribution to the recording and appreciation of the built environment." He now lives and works in a mill overlooking the slate mining town of Blaenau Ffestiniog, where he has an exhibition each summer which records the surrounding slate landscape.

Margarette Golding

The Inner Wheel is one of the largest Women's Service Organisations in the world, with over 100,000 members in more than 100 countries. It has grown to this size from very modest beginnings in Manchester in the 1920s. Inner Wheel was founded by Mrs Margarette Golding, who was its great inspiration and who steered the new organisation on its way in its early days.

The particular link with here is that she was born in Blaenau Ffestiniog, at 134 High Street, and spent the first 9 years of her life there. She was the first child of her parents, William Graianfryn Owen and his wife Sarah, who were married in the Baptist Chapel in Porthmadog in 1881. This chapel is now closed but the building can still be seen on leaving Porthmadog, going towards Tremadog, on the right hand side of the road just past the War Memorial Hill.

Her father had a lifelong career in the gas industry, progressing from being described as a "fitter" to positions of seniority and responsibility. It was one of these promotions that lead to Margarette and her family moving away from Blaenau Ffestiniog when she was 9. She never returned to live, though she retained fond and family links with this area throughout her life. She died, after a lengthy period of ill health, in 1939.

The Porthmadog Inner Wheel Club was founded in 1942.

WORKING WITH THE COMMUNITY

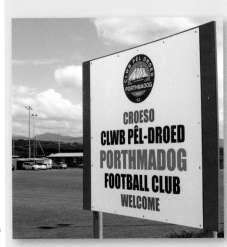

Roger Dimmick

Porthmadog FC

We are proud to be one of the major sponsors for Porthmadog Football Club, one of the oldest in Wales, being founded in 1884. Their ground is called Y Traeth, and is located on estuary land reclaimed by the construction of the Cob embankment. They play in the Huws Gray Alliance league which is the second level in the Welsh Football pyramid system. The club is a vibrant community with its own academy. Visitors are always very welcome to Y Traeth with its stunning views and friendly clubhouse. It is accessed from the Porthmadog bypass and can be seen clearly from both the main road and passing trains on the Welsh Highland Railway. To find out more about the club, log on to their website... **www.porthmadogfc.com.**

Andrew Thomas

We also take an active part in the local Chambers of Commerce - which benefits local shops and attractions, as well as our customers. We frequently attend events around the country and use this to promote our local area. We shop locally whenever we can, be it curtains made in Blaenau Ffestiniog for the new carriage, locally-sourced beer on the train or using local contractors for some of the major engineering projects we do. We hope you will follow our lead and shop locally too during your visit.

The Ffestiniog & Welsh Highland Railways are pleased to be an active part of this very special area of Wales and the communities along the way.

Jon March

Blaenau Station and Ysgol Maenofferen.

Unlike most of our other stations which are on their original site, Blaenau Ffestiniog Station was built in the early 1980s to provide a joint station with the Conwy Valley Line which runs all the way to Llandudno on the coast. As a more modern style station set in a town environment, it lacks the charm of some of our others - but that is changing, thanks to the hard work of our 'station adoption' team.

The team consists of two parts. A group of local residents have formed a loyal band who clean the station each day, paint and generally keep an eye on things. They are joined by a local primary school - Ysgol Maenofferen - whose boundary wall is shared with the station. The children love coming to plant bulbs and flowers and their artwork is displayed on both stations in the form of large murals and safety posters. This uplifting project has been part led by Arriva Trains Wales who have provided flower tubs and plants and have worked with the children to teach them about safety and good conduct. They have even written a song about the trains, and we can often find an excuse to get everybody out for a good sing song.

Jon March

SLATE - WHAT IS IT?

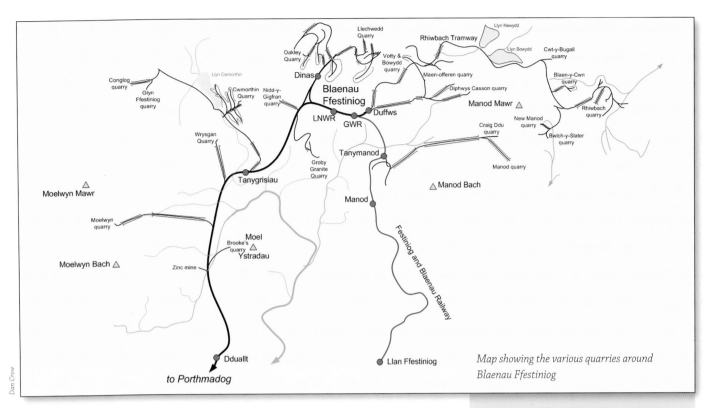

Dan Crow

Map showing the various quarries around Blaenau Ffestiniog

The Blaenau Ffestiniog beds of Ordovician blue-grey slate were created about 500 million years ago. They are therefore about 100 million years younger than the purple slate beds of the Caernarfon area. Slate is stone for the second time round! Countless hundreds of millions of years of wind, rain and chemical reaction eroded the world's first rocks, washing the resultant mud into the sea. There the tiny particles built up into layers of clay several hundred feet thick. Later volcanic action created folds in the earth's crust, heaving new mountains out of the seabed, with accompanying compression and movement making all the particles lie in the same direction. Heat from volcanic gases and lava caused some of the mineral particles to make new chemical combinations, especially minute flat ribbon-like particles of mica, which account for about 55% of the natural bulk of Blaenau Ffestiniog slate.

Mica crystals measure a virtually invisible 1/2000th of an inch in length and 1/6000th of an inch in thickness. Their presence gives Blaenau slate most of its universally prized properties, notably the fineness to which it can be split. At the London Exhibition of 1862, John W. Greaves, founder of the Llechwedd slate quarry, won a medal with slates 10ft long and 1ft wide, but only 1/16th of an inch thick. At a competition in 1872 everyone marvelled when a Llechwedd quarryman split a block 2½ inches thick into 45 layers. Today it is common-place for splitters to produce about 35 sheets per inch when making delicate slate ornaments, such as fans, using a chisel adapted from a table knife and blocks of the exceptionally fine quality Old Vein slate.

How Did the Slate Come Down the Mountain?

The slate industry would not have been able to develop without tramways; they provided cheap and efficient transport when often the only alternative was horse-drawn wagons over appalling roads. However, to enable tramways to function in mountainous areas a system was required to overcome sudden changes in height. The balanced inclined plane was the usual means of achieving this. An incline is a steeply sloped double-tracked formation with two ropes around a drum at the top. One of the ropes is attached to a number of loaded wagons at the top of the plane and the other rope fastened to a line of empty wagons at the bottom. By skilful use of the brake on the drum, the loaded wagons going down haul up the empty wagons - the two rakes passing halfway.

Another method of transporting product or waste was the 'Blondin' - named after the famous trapeze artist. A wire rope was strung between two towers across a pit and a truck was lowered or raised from the workings beneath using steam or electrical power.

In the slate industry's heyday there were over 500 balanced inclines in operation. The last incline of this type was taken out of use in 1976 at Maenofferen Quarry in Blaenau Ffestiniog. A good example of an incline is seen just before the train passes Glan y Pwll, on your left. At the top may be seen the supporting walls of the now collapsed drumhead around which the two ropes were wound. Inclines of this length only became practicable after the invention of steel ropes.

Courtesy A & G Hatherill

ENJOYING THE COUNTRYSIDE

Roger Dimmick

Roger Dimmick

Bruce Brayne

Above: *The magnificent Snowdon range of mountains seen across the still waters of the flooded Afon Glaslyn.*

There are many fine walking and cycling routes around the Ffestiniog Railway. The trains provide an excellent way to launch out for a day's exploration of the surrounding countryside. There are footpaths from Tan y Bwlch station to Croesor and to Dduallt – and on to Tanygrisiau. It's best to purchase an Ordnance Survey map of the area, on sale in our shops, or one of the many handy walking guide books – these will help you in choosing a walk that suits you and your abilities. Please remember that you should always equip yourselves properly if hiking in the mountains; even in summer it can turn cold and wet without a moment's notice. As can be seen from the map opposite, there are many footpaths around Blaenau Ffestiniog of varying difficulties for the casual or more seasoned hiker. The North Wales Coastal Path also passes near to Minffordd at Portmeirion.

The railway also links up with the cycleway, Lôn Ardudwy, from The Cob, Porthmadog, to Barmouth, which follows minor coastal roads. Forestry Commission Wales has established its Mountain Biking Centre at Coed y Brenin. Lôn Las Eifion runs from Bryncir to Caernarfon, finishing next to the Welsh Highland Railway station. A good day out is to cycle from Porthmadog to Caernarfon and bring the bikes back with you on the Welsh Highland Railway train.

Roger Dimmick

Roger Dimmick

Bruce Brayne

Huw Jenkins

Walking and cycling can get you up close and personal with the glorious environment of North Wales, but not everyone has the physical ability to take part in such strenuous activity. However, you can leave your car behind and travel in our trains. Although we burn fossil fuels, one train can carry over a hundred passengers – offsetting many car journeys. You can relax and the whole family can travel together and view the splendid countryside from the large panoramic windows. In fact, with the payment of a small supplement you can travel in our Observation Car; this is located at the rear of the train and affords uninterrupted views of Snowdonia on the up train to Blaenau Ffestiniog. On the way down you can see the engine as it negotiates the sharp curves whilst running down the valley. There are fine views of the Afon Dwyryd past Portmeirion with Harlech Castle in the distance.

There is much flora and fauna to be seen from the train. It's not just the rhododendrons in the spring – there is the beautiful sessile oak woodland near Tan y Bwlch, a glimpse maybe of a feral goat high up above Dduallt, buzzards, ravens, wildflowers and fabulous waterfalls and streams – all teeming with life. From The Cob can be seen Snowdon, Cnicht and the Moelwyn mountains in the distance, with hundreds of wading birds in the Traeth on the seaward side and in the Glaslyn marshes.

The railway has been pleased to be able to help the Forestry Commission with its logging activities in the mountains by transporting timber by train to Minffordd for transhipment.

The Ffestiniog Railway is part of a partnership to protect the local environment, working with the Countryside Council for Wales, the Snowdonia National Park Authority and Gwynedd Council.

49

PRESERVING OUR HERITAGE:
A BRIEF HISTORY OF THE FFESTINIOG RAILWAY

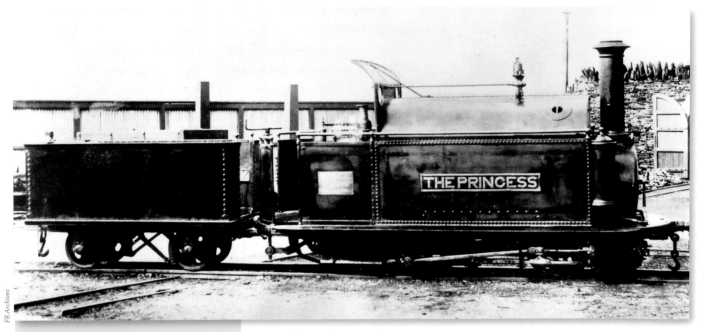

FR Archives

Above: 'The Princess' *in Boston Lodge works in 1887. This locomotive was one of the first batch delivered to the Ffestiniog Railway in 1863 by George England.*

Vintage carriages

The Ffestiniog Railway has a marvellous collection of vintage carriages. Some of these date back to the mid 1860s. In 1865, the FR was the first narrow gauge railway in Britain to be authorised by the Government to operate passenger trains - and the first in Britain to introduce iron-framed bogie carriages.

There is also a set of carriages in the livery of the 'Colonel Stephens' era' of the 1930s – as well as more recent items. These have all been restored by our team of craftsmen and women in our own carriage works at Boston Lodge.

Roger Dimmick

In the late 1700s, William Madocks, the member of Parliament for Boston in Lincolnshire, who had strong family links with the North Wales gentry, acquired property near Tremadog and began to carry out various projects to reclaim farm land from the Glaslyn estuary. The culmination of this work was his construction, between 1808 and 1811, of the great embankment now known as The Cob. By doing so he unwittingly set off a chain of events which have changed the entire character of this part of North Wales. By diverting the course of the Afon Glaslyn he created the conditions under which it scoured out a new natural harbour and thus altered the transport and trade links in the area.

The new harbour at Port Madoc had a deep enough draught to berth small ocean-going sailing ships, which could carry much larger amounts of slate than could be got to the port by the primitive means used until then. Something more efficient than pack-mules, carts and sledges was required. The answer was a narrow-gauge horse tramway, the fore-runner of today's Ffestiniog Railway.

Up until the advent of the railway, in the 1830s, slate had been transported from the quarries around Blaenau Ffestiniog to the sea by means of pack-mule and sledge to wharves on the Afon Dwyryd. These wharves, which are still visible today, were transhipment sites where the slate was loaded onto small boats which headed down-river. Near what is now Portmeirion, the slate was transferred to larger ocean-going vessels for export all over the world.

In 1832 an Act of Parliament was passed conferring powers to construct a railway from Blaenau Ffestinog to Porthmadog – by now a thriving port. The line was duly constructed, using a ruling gradient which allowed trains to run downhill by gravity, in 1836. The empty wagons were hauled back uphill by horses.

In order to traverse the steep mountainsides, where sharp curves ruled out the normal size of railway hastily being constructed all over Britain in these times, a smaller, narrow gauge was chosen. James Spooner (1790-1856) was the engineer responsible for the planning and construction of the little line. James Spooner's son, Charles Easton Spooner (1818-1889), took over responsibility for the line in 1856 – and subsequently introduced steam engines in 1863 when it became clear that the horse and gravity methods employed hitherto could not keep pace with demand.

FR Archives

The rapid expansion of British towns and cities in the Victorian era gave rise to increased demand for slate to roof the houses and factories. Steam engines were certainly a cheaper solution to the capacity problems experienced by the line – as proposals to double the number of tracks would have necessitated huge engineering considerations. The original little engines, *Princess, Prince, Palmerston, Mountaineer, Welsh Pony* and *Little Giant,* were becoming too small to work the increasingly long trains required by the demand for slate. The seemingly unstoppable growth in traffic led to Robert Fairlie's design for an articulated double engine being built for the railway. It was a huge success as it was the equivalent of two engines (back to back) but was cheaper to run as it only required one crew. Ever since these locomotives have been known as "Double Fairlies". There are currently three of them in traffic.

Above: 'The Princess' *at Duffws, Blaenau Ffestiniog, c1872.*

Below: 'Merddin Emrys' *waits to leave Porthmadog Harbour station, October 2012.*

Catalin Munteanu

John Thomas Collection, NLW

Gravity trains

When the railway opened in 1836 all "down" trains were worked by gravity. The "up" trains were horse-hauled - the horses riding back down again in special dandy wagons. Passenger trains were initially run down the line under gravity; goods, followed by passengers, followed by the locomotive - probably to give a shove if required. This practice was very swiftly curtailed by the Board of Trade! The practice of running slate trains down by gravity continued right up to the start of WW2.

Gravity trains were reintroduced in 1986 as an attraction at a Gala. The number of wagons in the train increased over the years and after a grant from the Heritage Lottery Fund a train of 51 wagons was restored and ran during the Vintage Weekend, 2002. Since then many more wagons have been restored.

In 2010, gravity trains made their television debut in BBC's 'Countryfile' programme and in a special feature on the National Geographic channel.

The FR remained in the forefront of railway development for many years. Having, in 1865, become the first narrow gauge railway in Britain to be allowed to run passenger trains it went on to introduce Britain's first iron-framed bogie carriages in 1872 and matched other companies in the introduction of safety features such as continuous brakes and single-line train control equipment. It also continued to make good profits.

Unfortunately, during the early years of the 20th Century, the slate industry began to decline, a trend accelerated by the loss of the large and lucrative German markets during WW1. Passenger traffic, mainly tourists by the 1930s, ceased in 1939 at the outbreak of WW2. Slate traffic dwindled to a trickle and the railway closed entirely in 1946. Fortunately, being a statutory company (one authorised by its own Act of Parliament) it transpired that it was impossible for the management to abandon the railway without getting another Act of Parliament. This would have cost more than the scrap value of the track and equipment and everything was still in place, albeit derelict and very overgrown, in 1954, when a band of railway enthusiasts finally managed to gain control of the line and begin the task of restoration.

Top: 'Merddin Emrys' *at Duffws, Blaenau Ffestiniog, c1880.*

Below: *M.V. Florence Cooke at Porthmadog Harbour in 1956.*

Below Left: *Gravity train approaching Rhiw Goch Farm crossing, May 2010.*

Roger Dimmick

FR Archives

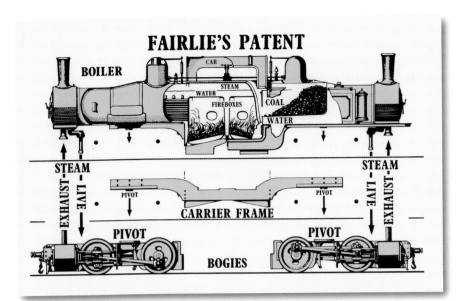

FAIRLIE'S PATENT

BOILER
CAB
STEAM
WATER
FIREBOXES
COAL
WATER

STEAM
EXHAUST
LIVE

STEAM
LIVE
EXHAUST

PIVOT
CARRIER FRAME
PIVOT

PIVOT
PIVOT
BOGIES

These railway enthusiasts formed the Ffestiniog Railway Society and the second half of the 20th Century saw the railway rise again. Alan Pegler managed to borrow enough money to be able to buy a majority shareholding – and the shares were placed in a special Trust set up for the purpose - the Ffestiniog Railway Trust. So a complicated, but interesting, legal arrangement was born, where the Festiniog Railway Company operates the railway, the majority of its shares are held by the Ffestiniog Railway Trust and the Ffestiniog Railway Society offers its support, both financial and with voluntary manpower.

People came to the area for holidays in much larger numbers and the growing number of railway enthusiasts during the 1950s produced a ready supply of volunteer labour. The revitalised railway owes much to the efforts and financial support of a large body of volunteers, without whom what you see around you today would not exist.

The railway was progressively re-opened, first to Boston Lodge in 1955 and then to Minffordd in 1956, Penrhyn in 1957 with Tan y Bwlch being reached in 1958.

Below: *Tan y Bwlch station in the 1960s.*

Below Right: *'David Lloyd George' leaving Blaenau Ffestiniog, May 2009.*

Geoff Plumb

Why is that Engine facing Both Ways?

The Ffestiniog Railway pioneered the world's first locomotives to be constructed with swivelling power bogies, which provide great power and allow much heavier trains to be handled without increasing manpower costs. The double Fairlie engines have long boilers with chimneys at both ends. Of immediately striking and endearing appearance, there are several still to be seen around the railway. As a reward for publicising his design, Robert Fairlie gave the FR free use of his patent and we are still building Fairlies today.

The current fleet comprises Merddin Emrys, built in 1879, Earl of Merioneth completed in 1979 and David Lloyd George, put into service in 1992. Livingston Thompson, built in 1885 and now thoroughly worn out, is on loan to the National Railway Museum in York. Taliesin is a single Fairlie, completed by the railway in 1999. It only faces one way, but has a swivelling power bogie just like its double-ended stable mates. All five of these engines were built in the company's own workshops at Boston Lodge.

FR Archives

Robert Francis Fairlie (1831-1885) designed the famous double-bogie articulated locomotives which were promoted on the Ffestiniog Railway in the late 1860s.

Roger Dimmick

53

FR Archives

Above: 'Welsh Pony' *at Duffws station, Blaenau Ffestiniog.*
Left: *Replica of the original enamelled works plate.*

Glenn Williams

Welsh Pony Restoration Project

'Welsh Pony' was one of the first steam locomotives to work on the Ffestiniog Railway, arriving from the George England works in London in 1867. Slightly larger than her sisters 'Prince' and 'Princess', she worked throughout the old company years, pulling trains on both Ffestiniog and Welsh Highland Railways. A true survivor, she continued to work through the poorer years, being maintained as best they could with the resources available.

In more recent times, she spent many years on a plinth outside Harbour Station, promoting her railway. Now, a major restoration project is underway to preserve this unique locomotive in time for her 150th birthday. Funds have been raised from many sources including a huge response from the general public who have put their small change in envelopes on the trains to save this little engine. Enough has been raised to allow work to start in earnest.

A new boiler is being built along with other significant parts, but it is a credit to her builders and those who cared for her years ago that many of the original parts can be reused. There is still a long way to go but in the caring hands of a new generation of engineers, she could be finished by the end of 2017.

Between 1957 and 1963, an electricity generating scheme had resulted in the line being flooded above Dduallt and the Deviation was built to restore the link through to Blaenau Ffestiniog. Trains to Dduallt re-started in 1968, but services to Blaenau Ffestiniog were not fully restored until the new joint station was opened in 1982. The new station was constructed on the site of the old GWR station and resulted in the closure of the old LNWR station, which was less central to the town. Blaenau Ffestiniog central station was a joint project with the Ffestiniog Railway, British Rail and Gwynedd County Council all working together to improve the amenity in this historic town.

As you journey up through the mountain scenery, take time to reflect on the marvel of the Georgian and Victorian engineering on which you are travelling. Most of the trackbed which carries the railway was hewn by hand from the mountains nearly two hundred years ago; the dry-stone walls and embankments, some of which are over sixty feet high, are still in good repair today. These are all maintained by a small band of paid staff and many volunteers who come to the railway every year.

We are lucky that more recent visionaries saw fit to save this railway from extinction. Maybe you'll see *Prince*, the world's oldest working steam locomotive, perhaps you'll sit in one of the world's earliest bogie carriages, or see our famous double-ended Fairlie locomotives. All this while you travel on the first narrow gauge railway in Britain authorised to carry fare-paying passengers!

It's not just the trains which form part of the heritage of this part of North Wales. There are other attractions as well. Portmeirion, Plas Brondanw and Llechwedd Slate Caverns are all within easy reach of the Ffestiniog Railway trains – as is our sister railway, the Welsh Highland Railway, which runs between Caernarfon and Porthmadog.

In 1863 the railway introduced steam locomotives and in 1865, the first passengers travelled on the line. The Ffestiniog Railway proved that useful trains could operate on such narrow, twisty tracks – and this concept has been exported to many other railways all over the world.

FFESTINIOG RAILWAY TIMELINE

1808-11 Building of the Cob

1832 FR Act of Parliament given Royal assent on 23 May

1836 Railway opens

1863 First steam engines

1865 Passenger services start

1869 First double Fairlie Locomotive, *Little Wonder*

1870 The International Commission conducts experiments on the FR

1871 Visit of General William Jackson Palmer

1872 First iron-framed bogie coaches in Britain

Exchange sidings built at Minffordd

1879 First locomotive built at Boston Lodge: Double Fairlie *Merddin Emrys*

1886 Double Fairlie *Livingston Thompson* built at Boston Lodge

1915 Boston Lodge Works becomes a munitions factory for the duration of WW1

1939 FR passenger services suspended in September as WW2 breaks out

1946 All services suspended

1951 The Bristol Meeting called by Leonard Heath Humphrys galvanises efforts to reopen the railway.

1954 Alan Pegler buys a controlling interest in the company and rebuilding of the railway commences.

1955 Passenger services restart between Porthmadog and Boston Lodge on 23 July. *Prince* back in service

1956 Services extended to Minffordd

1957 Services extended to Penrhyn, double Fairlie *Taliesin* (formerly *Livingston Thompson*) back in service

1958 Services extended to Tan y Bwlch

1962/3 *Linda* and *Blanche* purchased from the Penrhyn Quarry Railway

1965 Construction of the Dduallt-Tanygrisiau deviation line starts

1968 Services extended to Dduallt

1977 Trains run to a temporary terminus beside Llyn Ystradau

1978 Deviation completed, services extended to Tanygrisiau

1979 New double Fairlie locomotive *Earl of Merioneth* built at Boston Lodge

1982 Services extended to Blaenau Ffestiniog

1992 New double Fairlie locomotive *David Lloyd George* built at Boston Lodge

1999 New single Fairlie *Taliesin* built at Boston Lodge

2004/5 Golden Jubilee of the saving of the FR by enthusiasts

2007 175 year Celebrations

2011 200 year anniversary of The Cob

2013 150 years of steam locomotives on the Ffestiniog Railway

2015 150 years of carrying passengers on the Ffestiniog Railway

CAN I HELP THE FFESTINIOG RAILWAY?

Yes, you can! We always need more volunteers to help us. There are so many things to do, to suit people of all ages and abilities. The people pictured on these pages are mostly volunteers and some are paid staff who started out on the railway as volunteers. You could join them.

There are many jobs to do; some are glamorous, some are not! But they're all important to keeping the railway going. It's not just looking after the engines and carriages – we have many miles of track and a large number of buildings which need constant maintenance. We also have a huge collection of wagons, many of which are over a hundred years old.

Chris Parry

Of course, if you like dealing with people, there are many jobs that are in the public eye. We have several ticket offices, cafés and shops – all of which need volunteers to help us operate trains through most of the year. All trains need guards, firemen (and women!) as well as drivers. It takes quite a few years to learn to be an engine driver, so why not start now!

You can join the Ffestiniog Railway Society or the Heritage Group (see panels on page 60 for details). For more information on volunteering contact the Volunteer Resources Manager on 01766 516035 or email **tdoyle@ffwhr.com**

To help you we even have Hostels where you can stay at reduced rates if you're working on the railway. We look forward to seeing you.

Kids' Training Week

For twenty five years now the FR has operated a 'Kids' Training Week' during August. This is designed to give young volunteers, aged between 14 and 17, a taste of railway life. There are usually around 40 places for the young volunteers who stay locally in residential accommodation for the week, or live locally.

They are supported by adult volunteers who act as House parents and Project leaders. The adults always include a number of Kids Week graduates who return to share their experiences with the next generation.

Participation in the Week's activities results in the development of personal lifetime skills, self confidence, enhanced job prospects and recognised national qualifications. In order to be able to do this, the railway has worked to become an accredited training centre under the auspices of Agored Cymru.

Roy Woods

Roy Woods

WORK IN PROGRESS AT BOSTON LODGE

Andrew Thomas

Fitting the crankpins to Double Fairlie 'David Lloyd George's' new wheels using liquid nitrogen at minus 196 degrees centigrade; Boston Lodge works, July 2012.

'Lyd' being repainted in Southern Railway green livery, September 2011. Only three coats of varnish remain to be applied by Glenn Williams at Boston Lodge works.

Andrew Thomas

Roger Dimmick

Above: *We are proud of our Victorian heritage and our annual Vintage Weekend features authentic trains from throughout our history, a variety of costumed characters, sideshows, stands and stalls creating a marvellous atmosphere the whole family can enjoy.*

The Small Print
The Festiniog Railway Co. has made every effort to ensure the accuracy of information contained in this publication.
Not all of the establishments mentioned herein are open every day - it is wise to check beforehand, especially if you're planning to eat out!
Disclaimers: This publication does not contain a complete list of every accommodation or facility in the area and listing here does not necessarily constitute an endorsement.